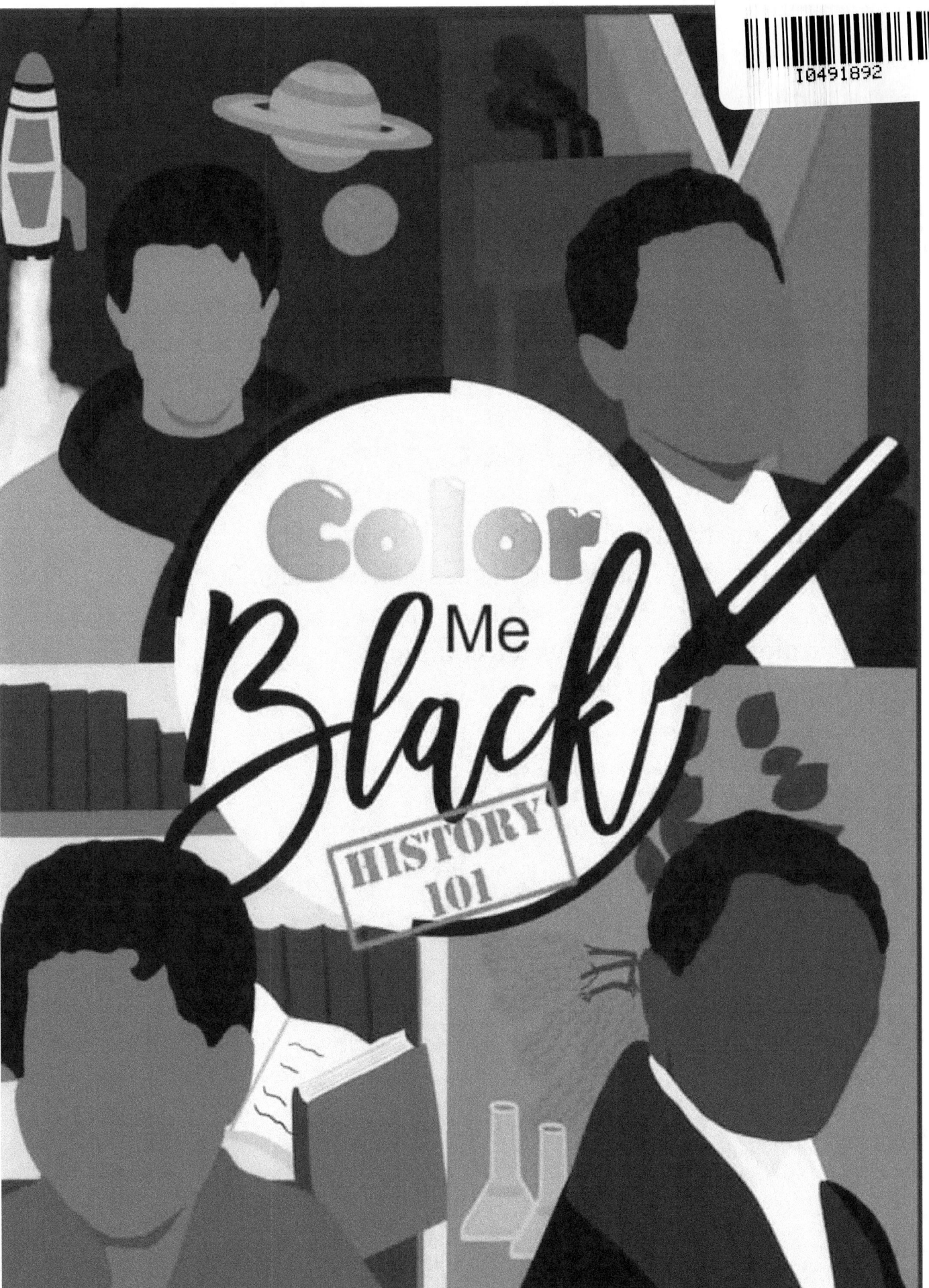

Copyright

Dedication

What does Black History Month mean to you?

Kamara Paige

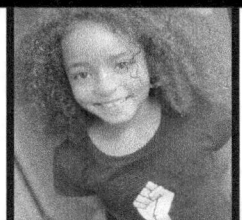

9 Years old , Des Moines,IA

It means everything because I'm black. It is about brown people that did good in our country.

Londyn Hartwell

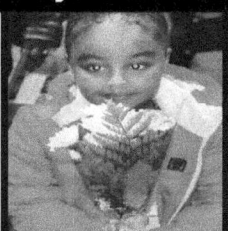

8 years old, Hampton, VA

It's a month for us to embrace our blackness.

Niah Floyd

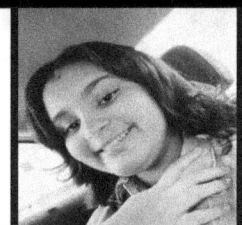

12 years old, Des Moines, IA

When you are black you don't get a lot of credit for stuff or even celebration. So Black History Month is one way of showing how we can be amazing and wonderful. Not always a threat to people. We need to be apprecaited more. We aren't ghost we are human too. Even though I'm still a kid, I know more about my culture than some adults do.

Ava Chanel Wilson

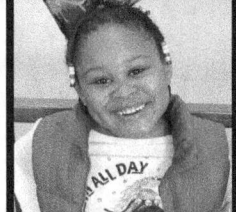

7 years old, Johnston, IA

Black History Month is a time where we get to learn about our lives as black people. I love it because I am learning about people that look like me.

Peyton Harrington

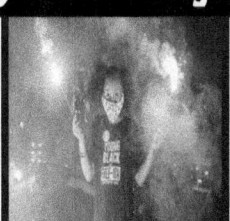

9 Years old , Des Moines,IA

"Black History is the beauty if black culture. I appreciate my black heritage, I love being black!"

Sojourner Truth
1797-1883

An African American woman that was born into slavery but escaped to freedom in 1826 with her daughter. She was a women's rights activist that became the first black woman to win a case against a white man in court to recover her son in 1828. "If women wanted any rights more than they's got, why don't they just take them, and not be talking about it" –Sojourner Truth

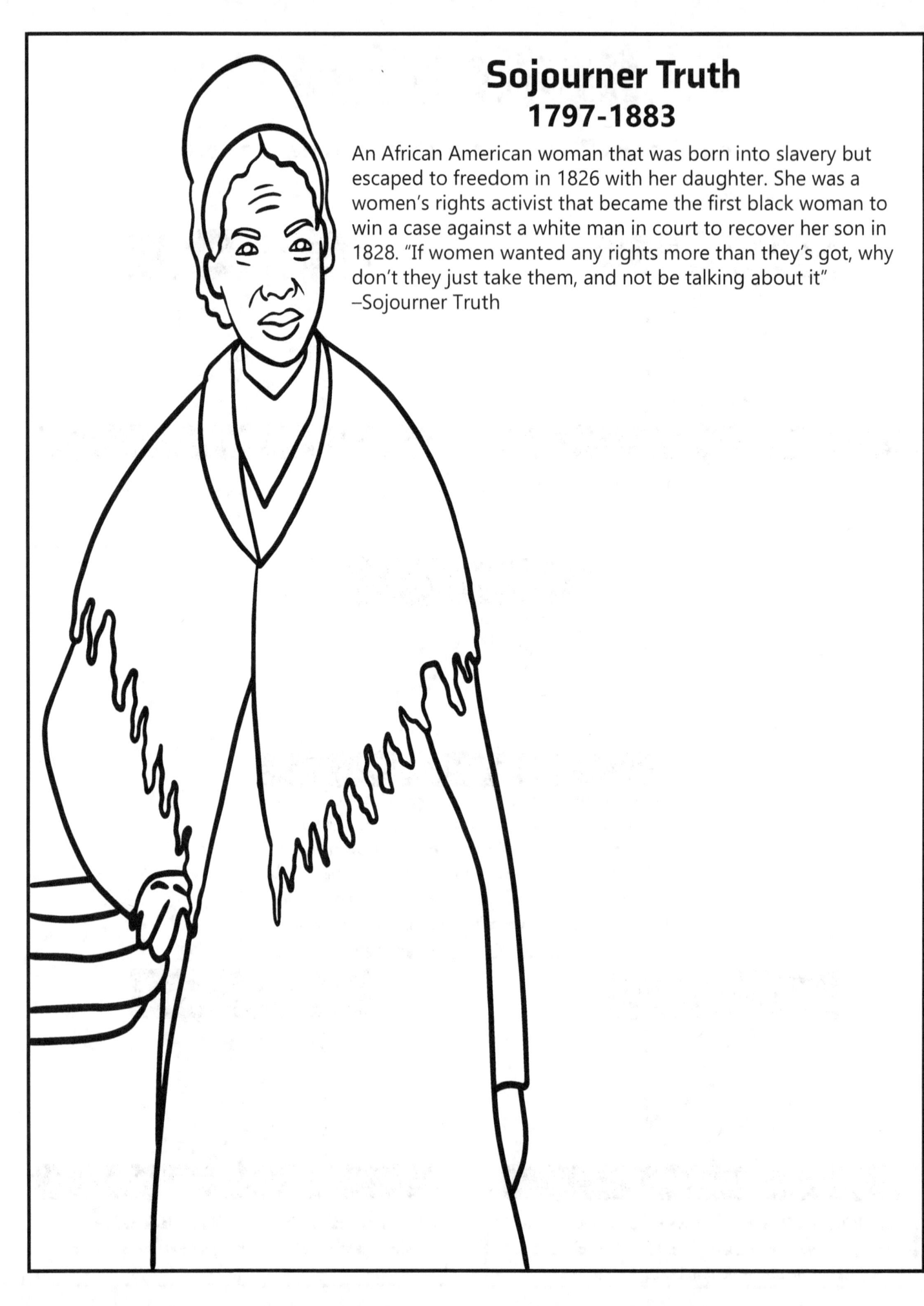

John Lewis
1940-2020

An African American man that was known as a leader and great civil rights activist. He participated in the Freedom Rides of 1961, and also spoke at The March on Washington in 1963. He led what was known as "Bloody Sunday" or March from Selma and was beaten severely. He was also elected and served as the United States House of Representatives for Georgia's 5th congressional district since 1987.

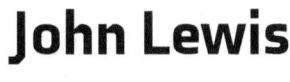

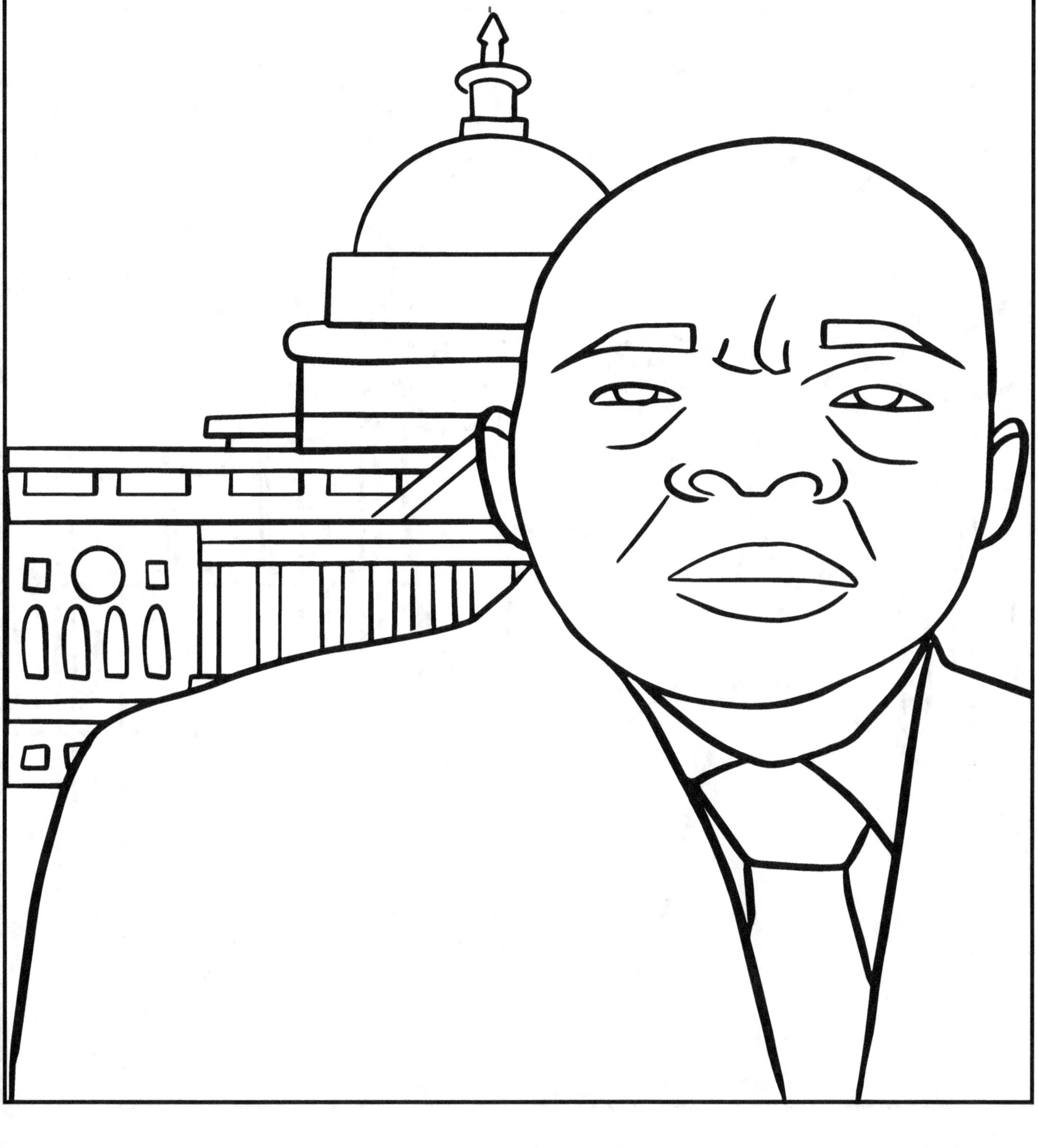

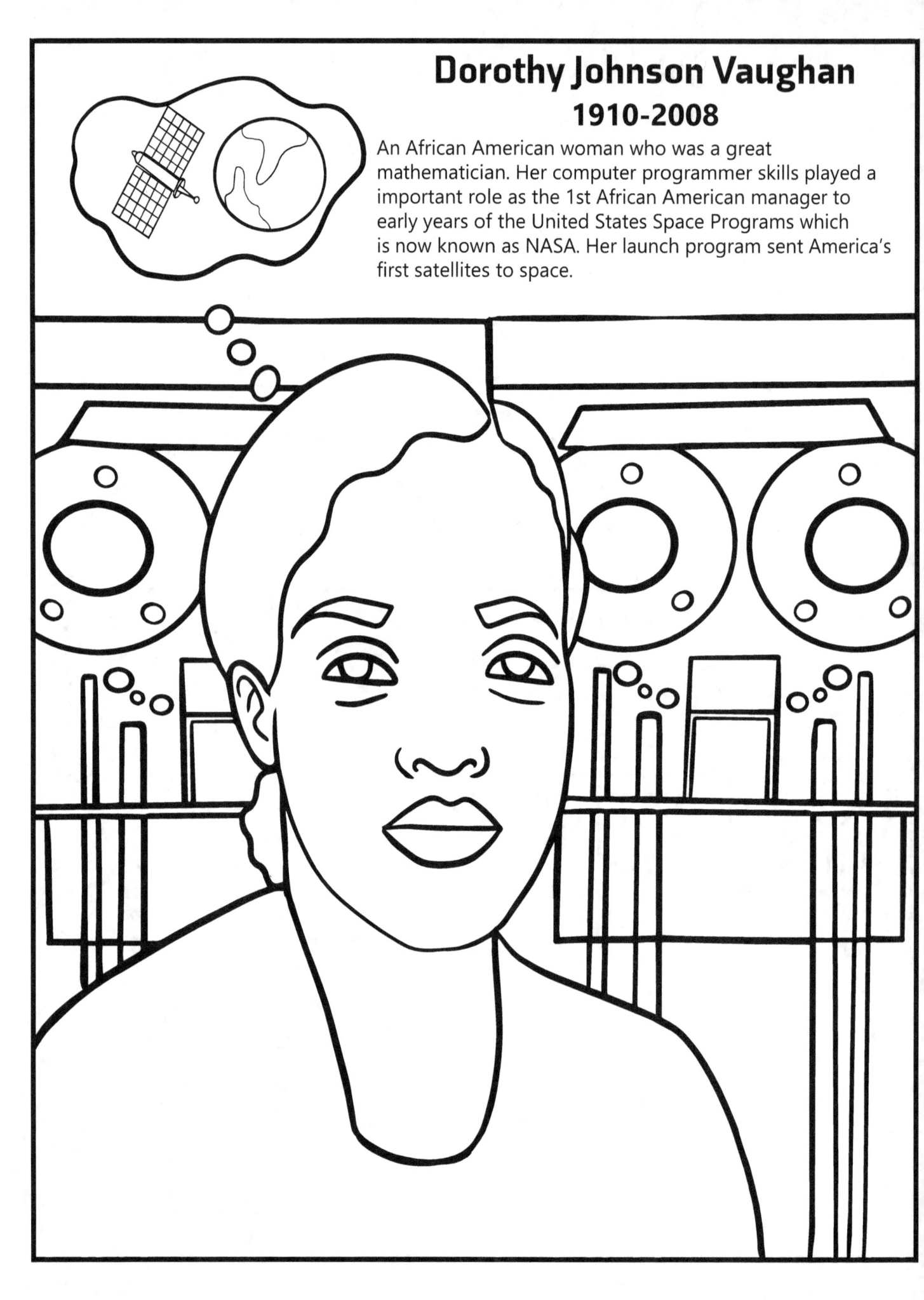

Dorothy Johnson Vaughan
1910-2008

An African American woman who was a great mathematician. Her computer programmer skills played a important role as the 1st African American manager to early years of the United States Space Programs which is now known as NASA. Her launch program sent America's first satellites to space.

Nelson Mandela
1918-2013

A South African revolutionary, political leader and philanthropist. He was the President of South Africa from 1994-1999. The first black head of state elected by democratic election. "We need to know with a fresh conviction that we all share a common humanity and that our diversity in the world is the strength for our future together" –Nelson Mandela

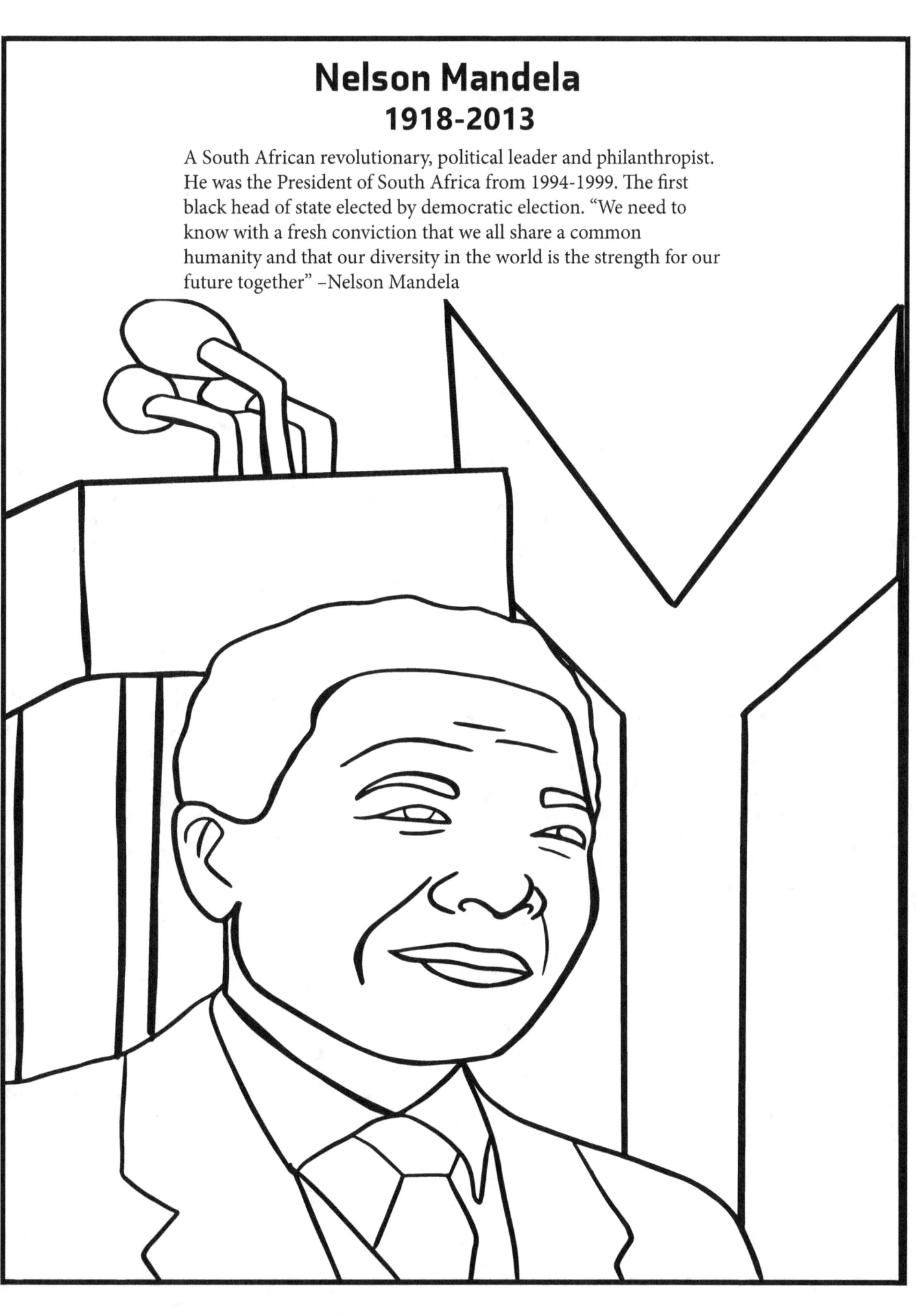

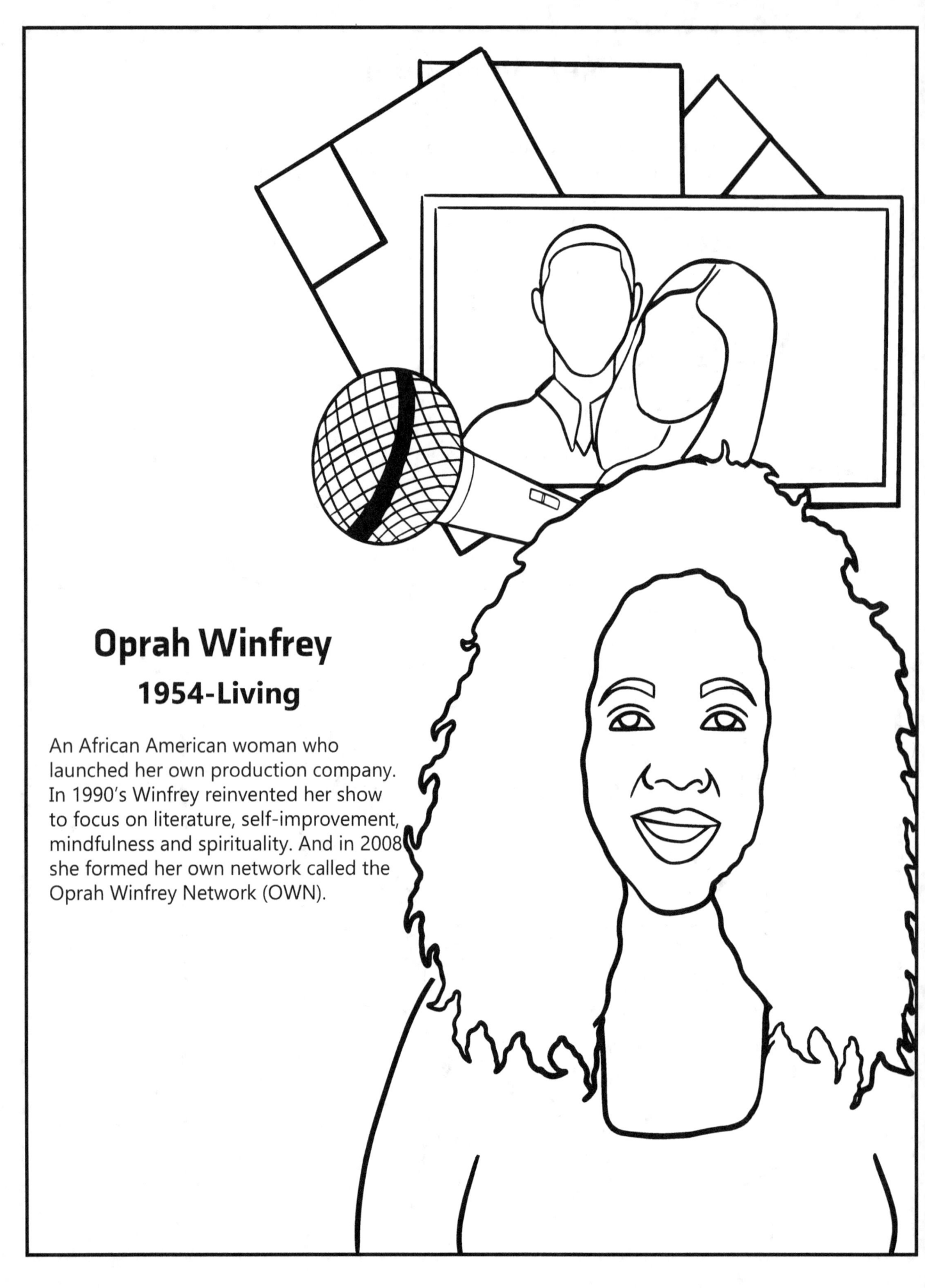

Oprah Winfrey

1954-Living

An African American woman who
launched her own production company.
In 1990's Winfrey reinvented her show
to focus on literature, self-improvement,
mindfulness and spirituality. And in 2008
she formed her own network called the
Oprah Winfrey Network (OWN).

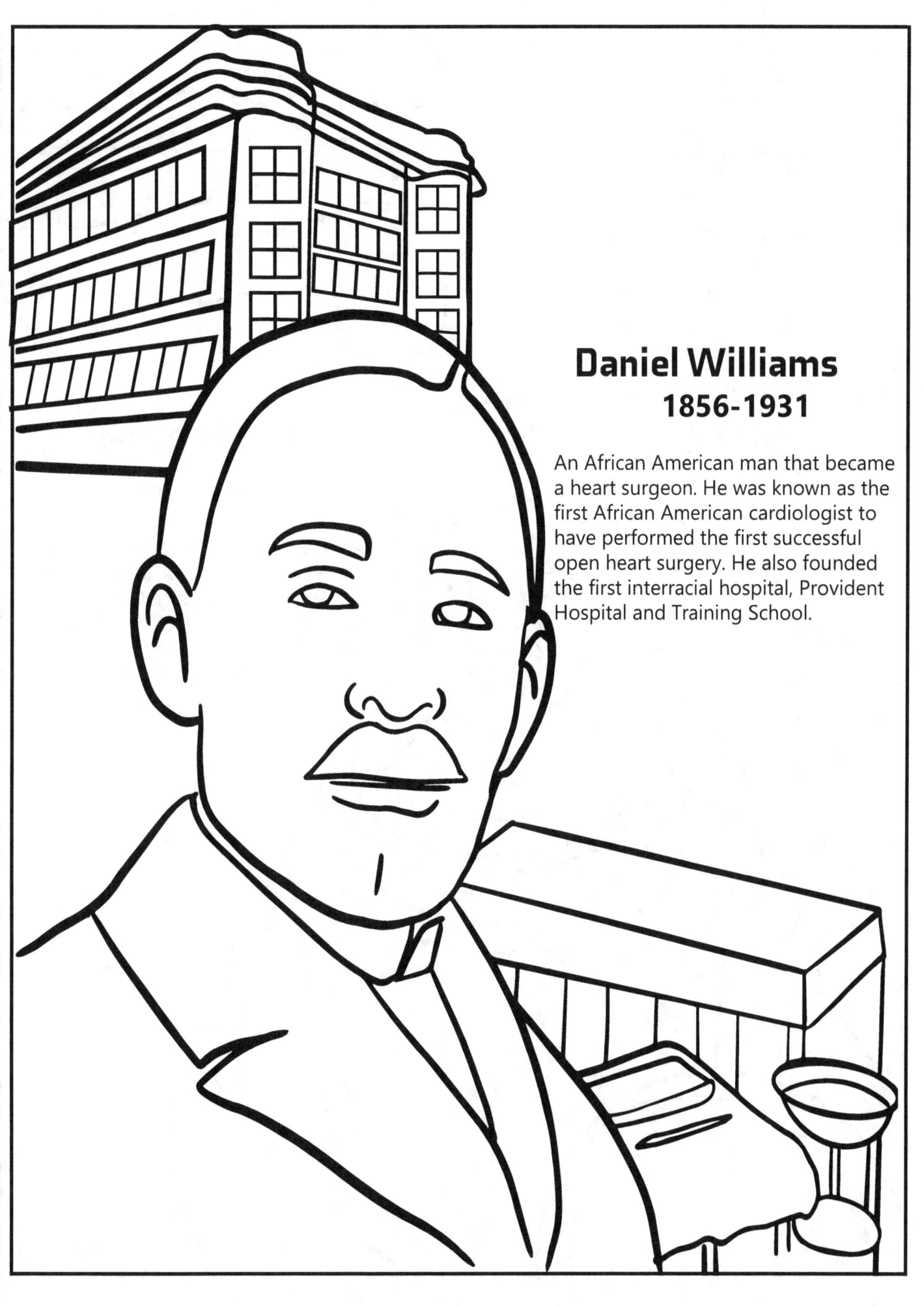

Daniel Williams
1856-1931

An African American man that became a heart surgeon. He was known as the first African American cardiologist to have performed the first successful open heart surgery. He also founded the first interracial hospital, Provident Hospital and Training School.

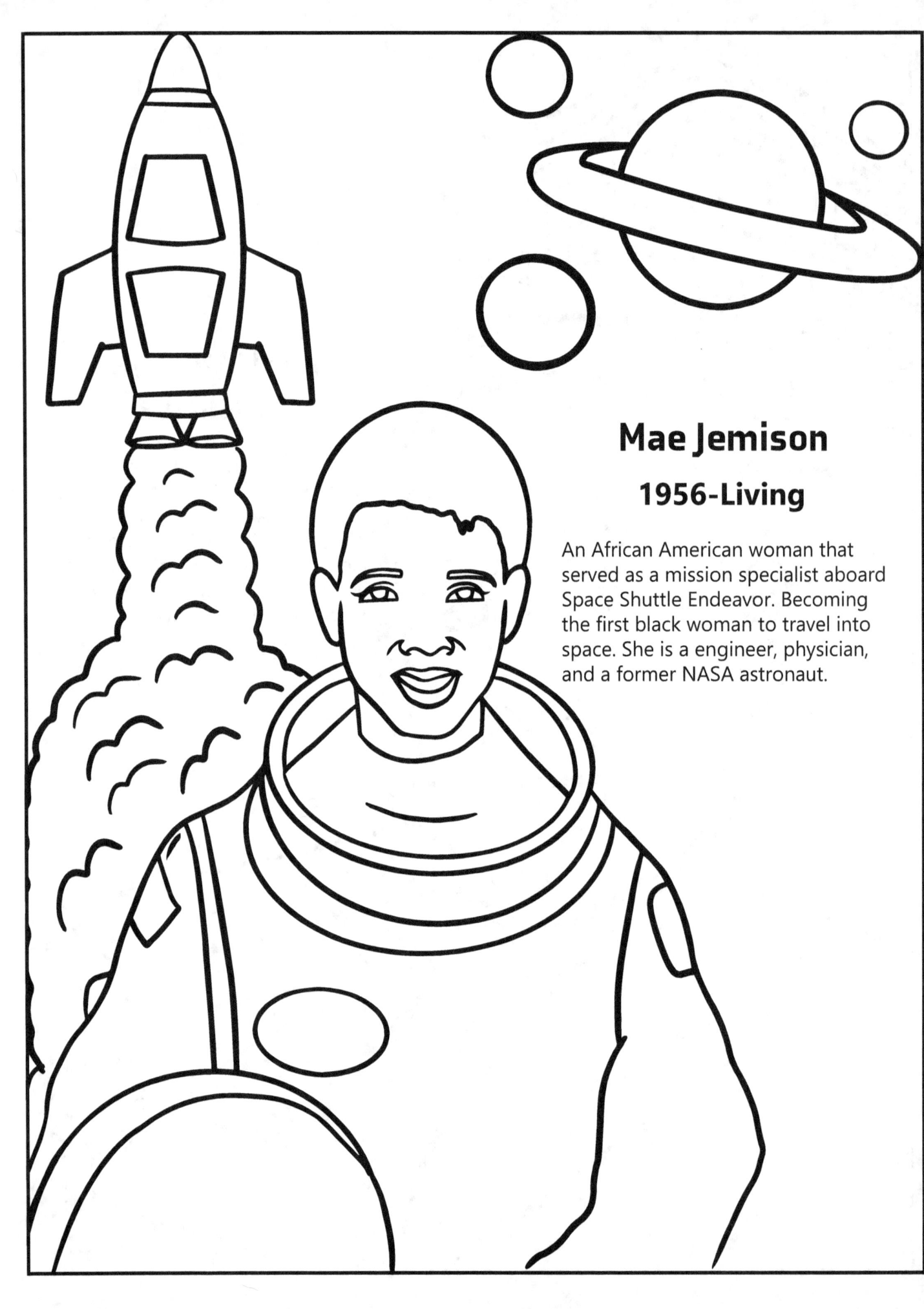

Mae Jemison

1956-Living

An African American woman that served as a mission specialist aboard Space Shuttle Endeavor. Becoming the first black woman to travel into space. She is a engineer, physician, and a former NASA astronaut.

Langston Hughes
1902-1967

An African American man who was an early innovator of the new literary art form called "
jazz poetry". He was known as a leader of the Harlem Renaissance. Hughes was a poet, social activist, novelist, and play writer.

"I too, sing America.
I am the darker brother.
They send me to eat in the kitchen
When company comes,
But I laugh,
And eat well,
And grow strong.
Tomrrow,
I'll be at the table
When company comes,
Nobody'll dare
Say to me,
"Eat in the kitchen."
Then,
Besides,
They'll see how beautiful I am
And be ashamed-
I, too, am America.
–Langston Hughes

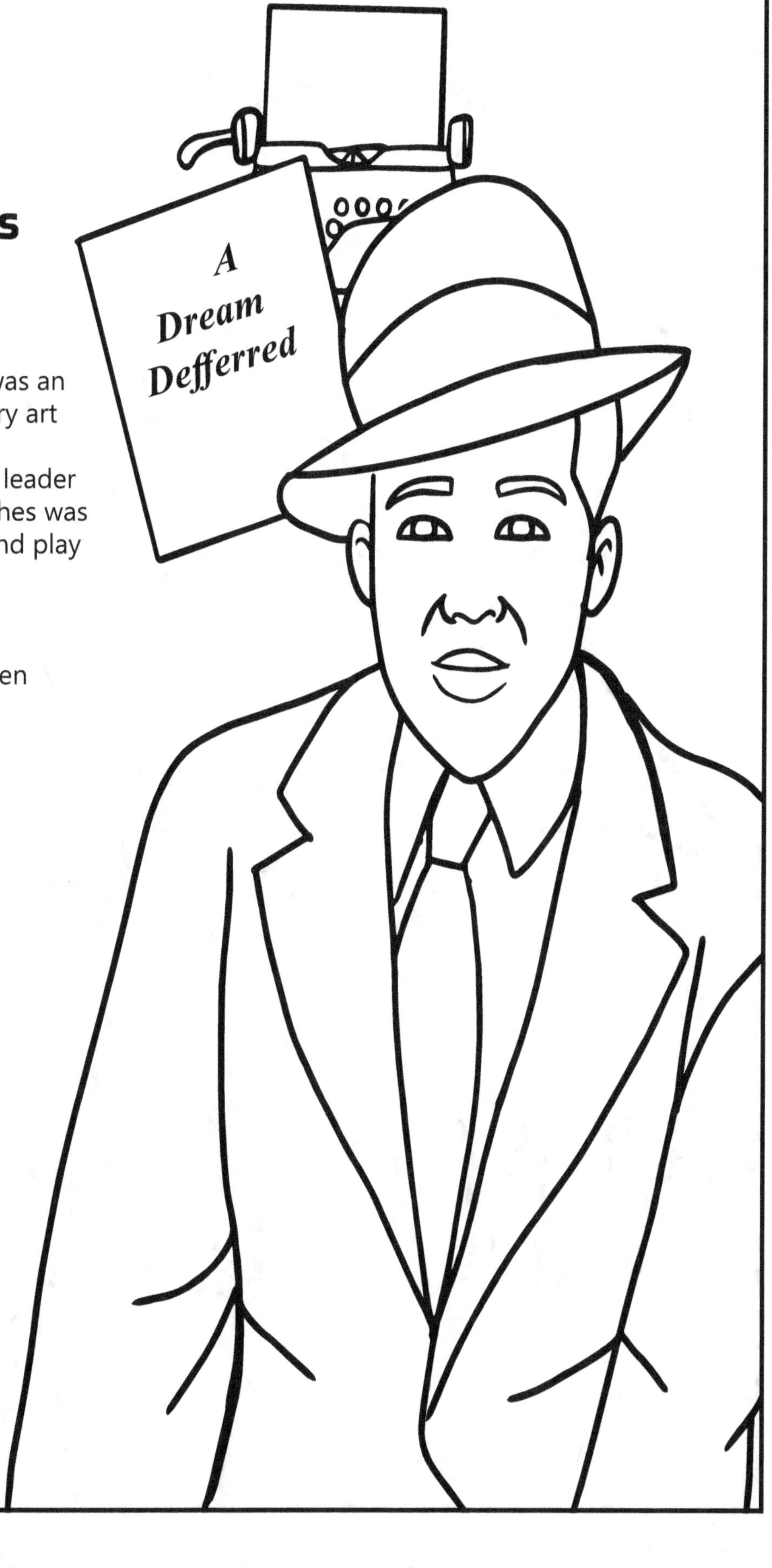

A Dream Defferred

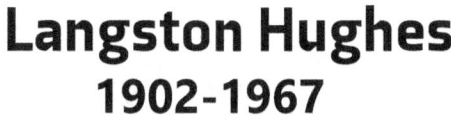

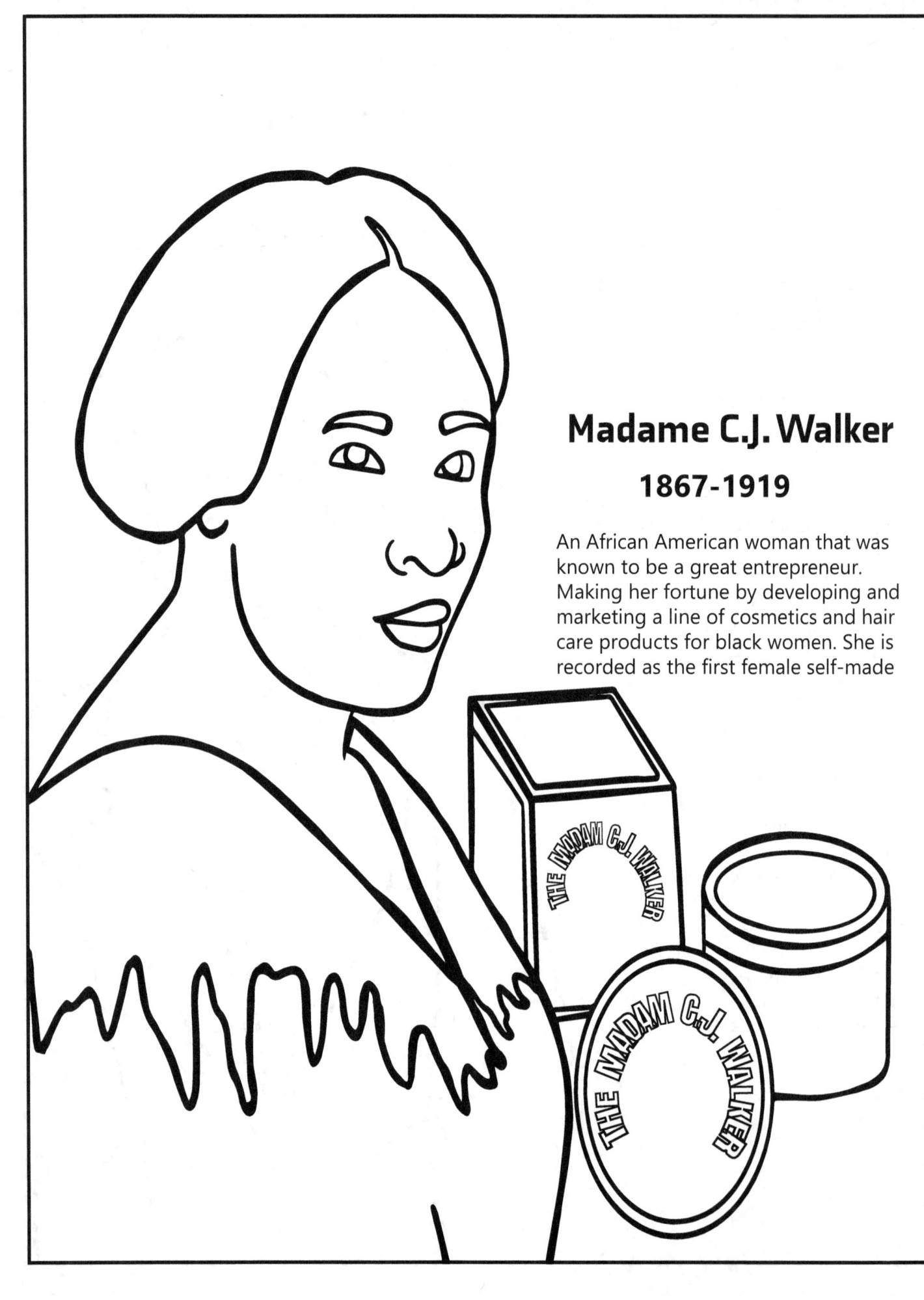

Madame C.J. Walker

1867-1919

An African American woman that was known to be a great entrepreneur. Making her fortune by developing and marketing a line of cosmetics and hair care products for black women. She is recorded as the first female self-made

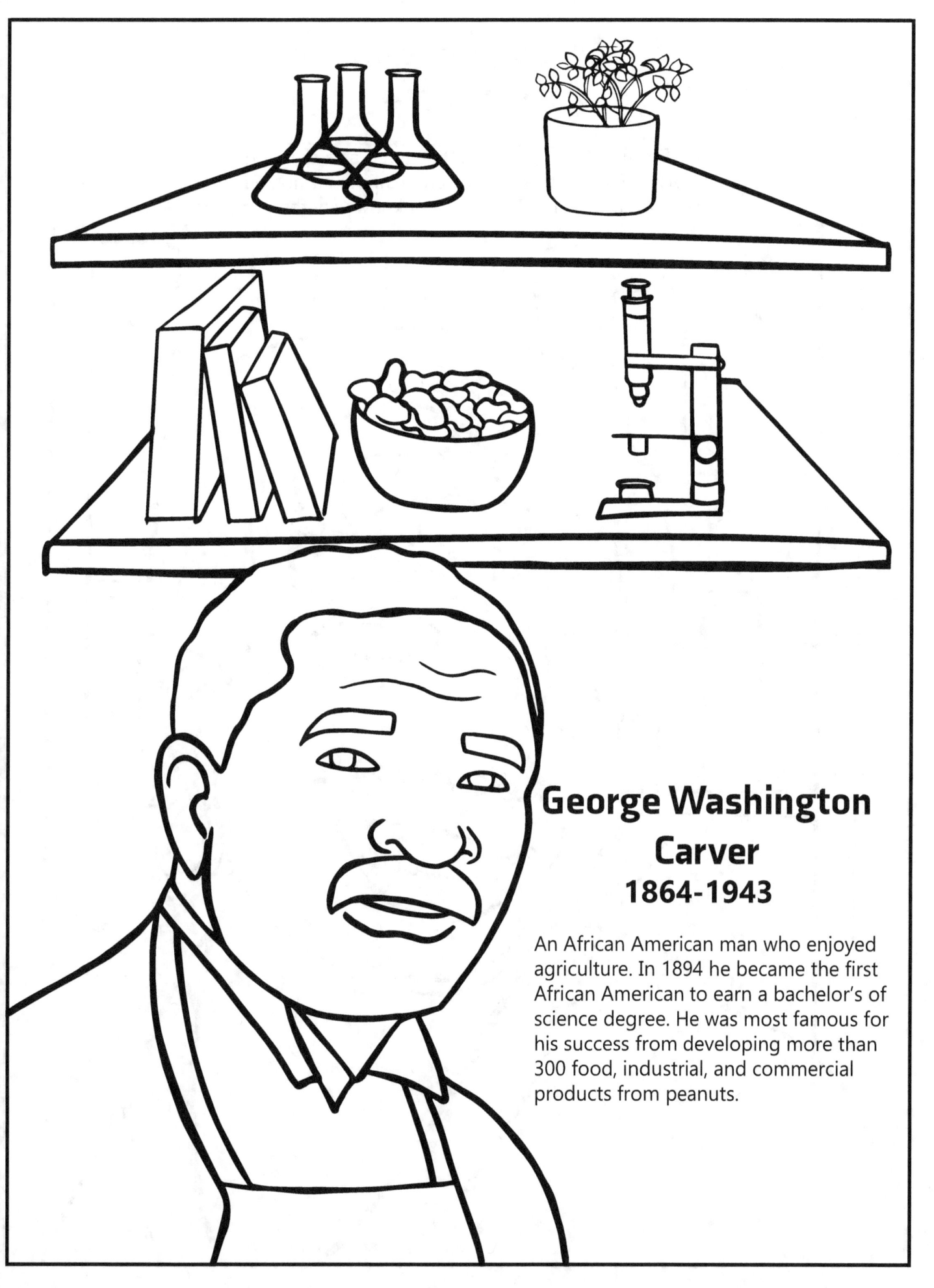

George Washington Carver
1864-1943

An African American man who enjoyed agriculture. In 1894 he became the first African American to earn a bachelor's of science degree. He was most famous for his success from developing more than 300 food, industrial, and commercial products from peanuts.

Maya Angelou
1928-2014

An African American woman that acted as a civil rights activist, a famous poet and award winning author. One of her most famous books is called "I know why the cage bird sings".

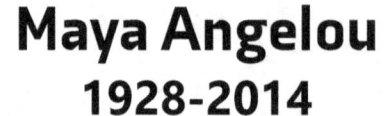

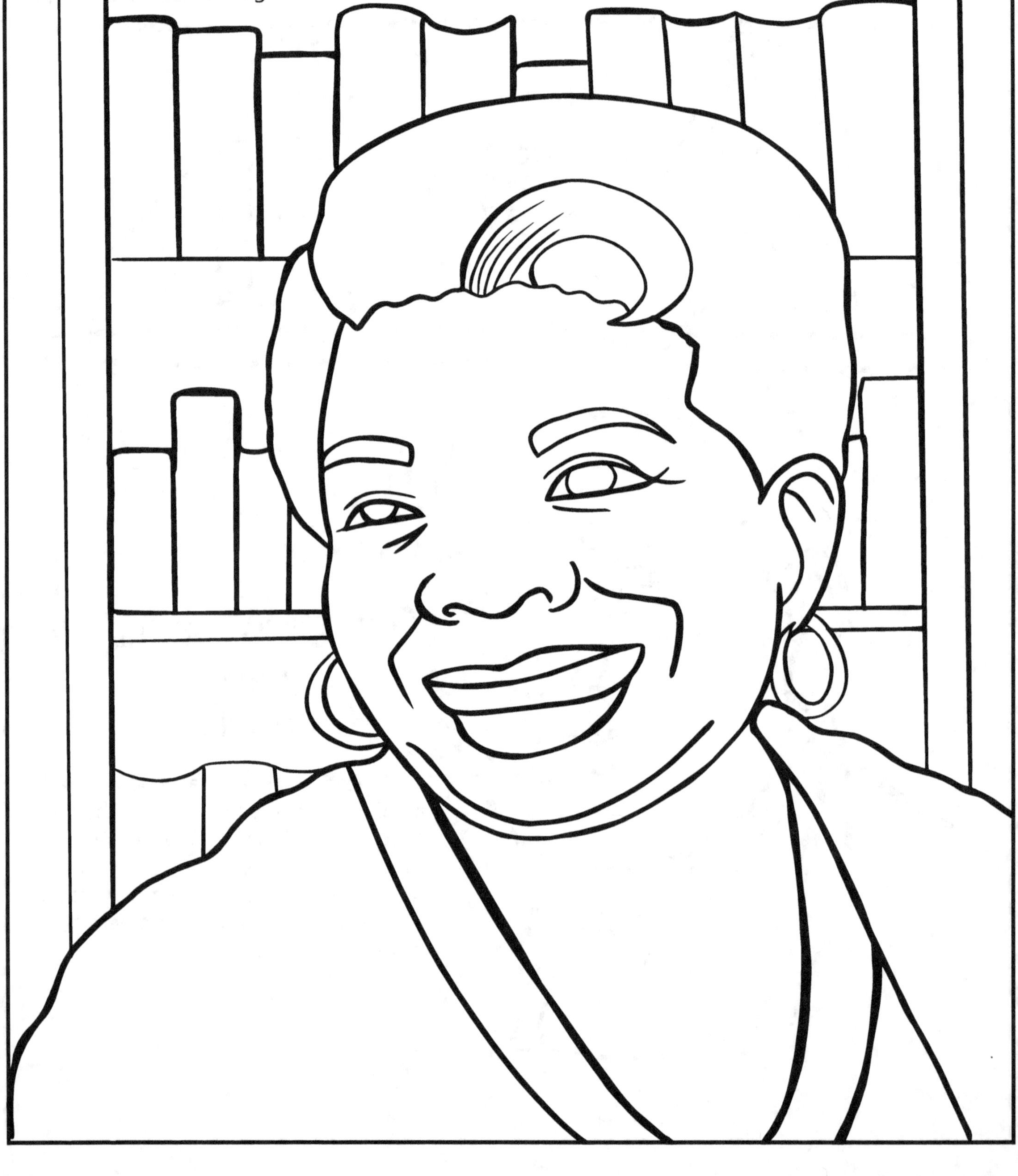

Jackie Robinson

1919-1972

An African American man that became the first to play in Major League Baseball in modern times. Breaking all lines of color when Robinson started 1st base playing for the Brooklyn Dodgers in 1947.

Career Stats: AB(at bat) 4877   **H(hits)** 1518   **HR(home runs)** 137 **BA(batting average)** 311

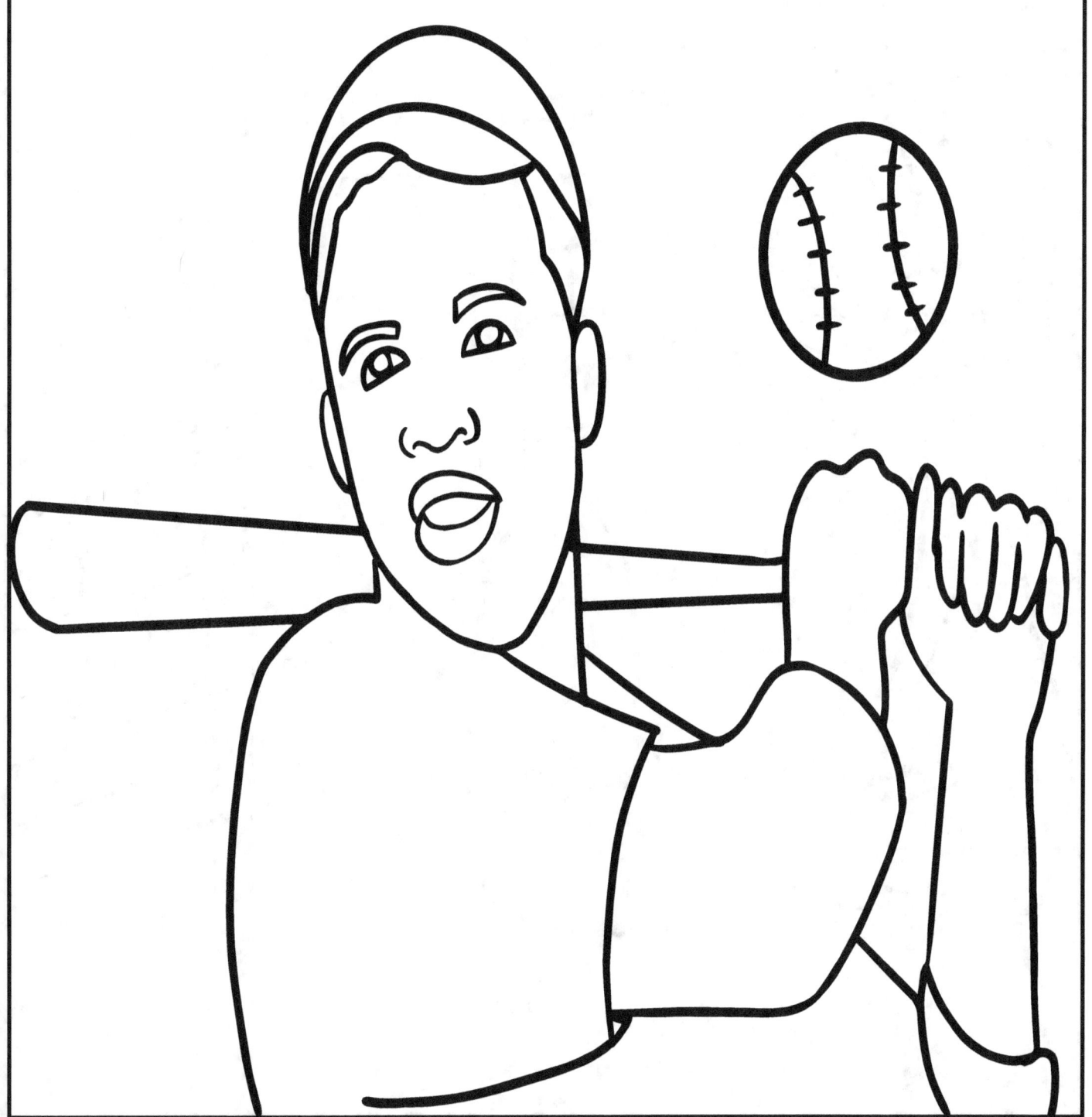

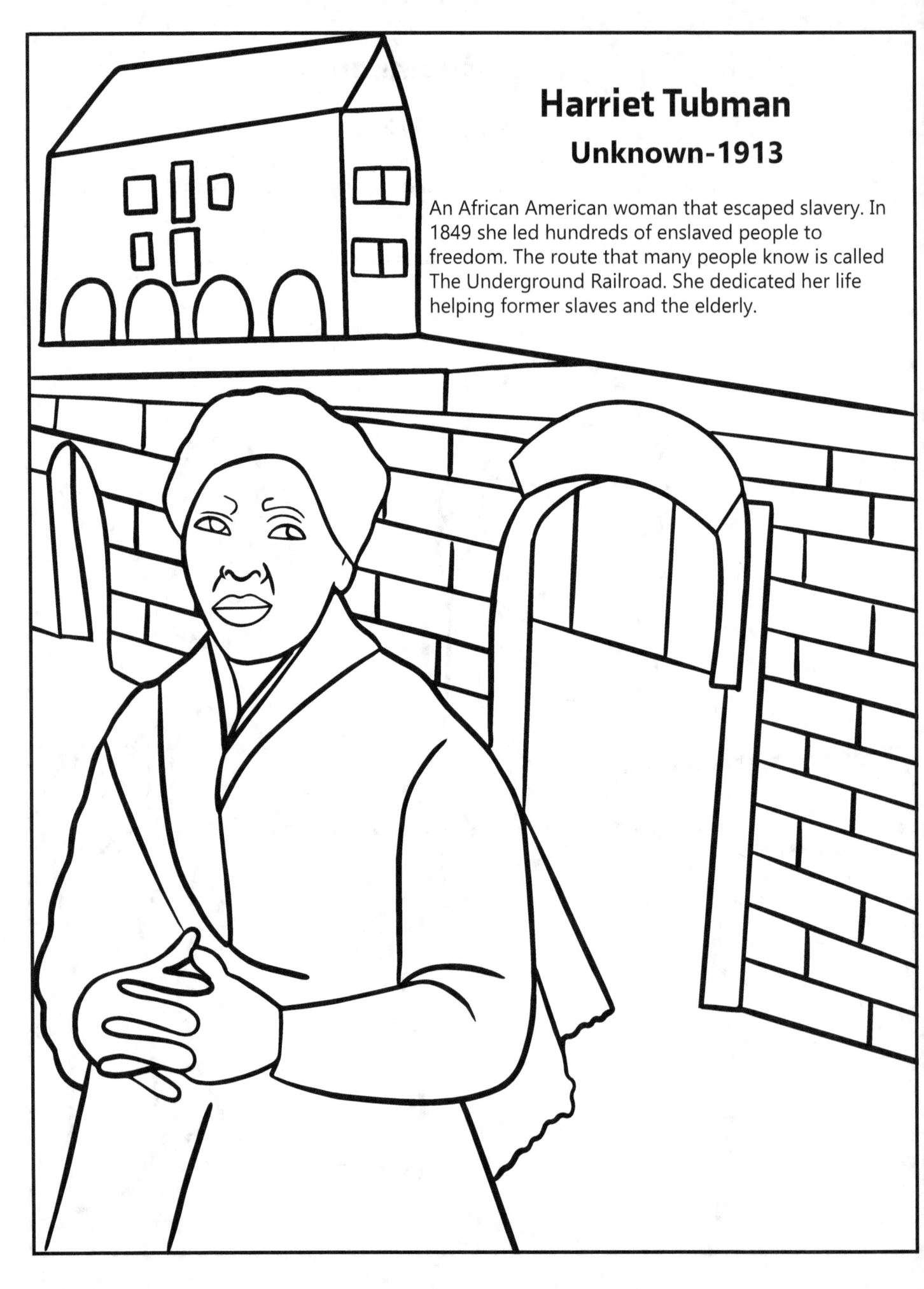

Harriet Tubman
Unknown-1913

An African American woman that escaped slavery. In 1849 she led hundreds of enslaved people to freedom. The route that many people know is called The Underground Railroad. She dedicated her life helping former slaves and the elderly.

Muhammad Ali

1942-2016

An African American man that was known as "the greatest" professional boxer in America. A heavy weight champion with 56 win record. Ali got drafted into the military in 1967 and refused to serve because of his practice of Muslim religious beliefs.

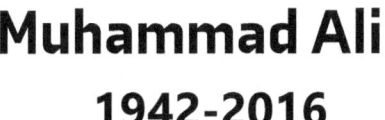

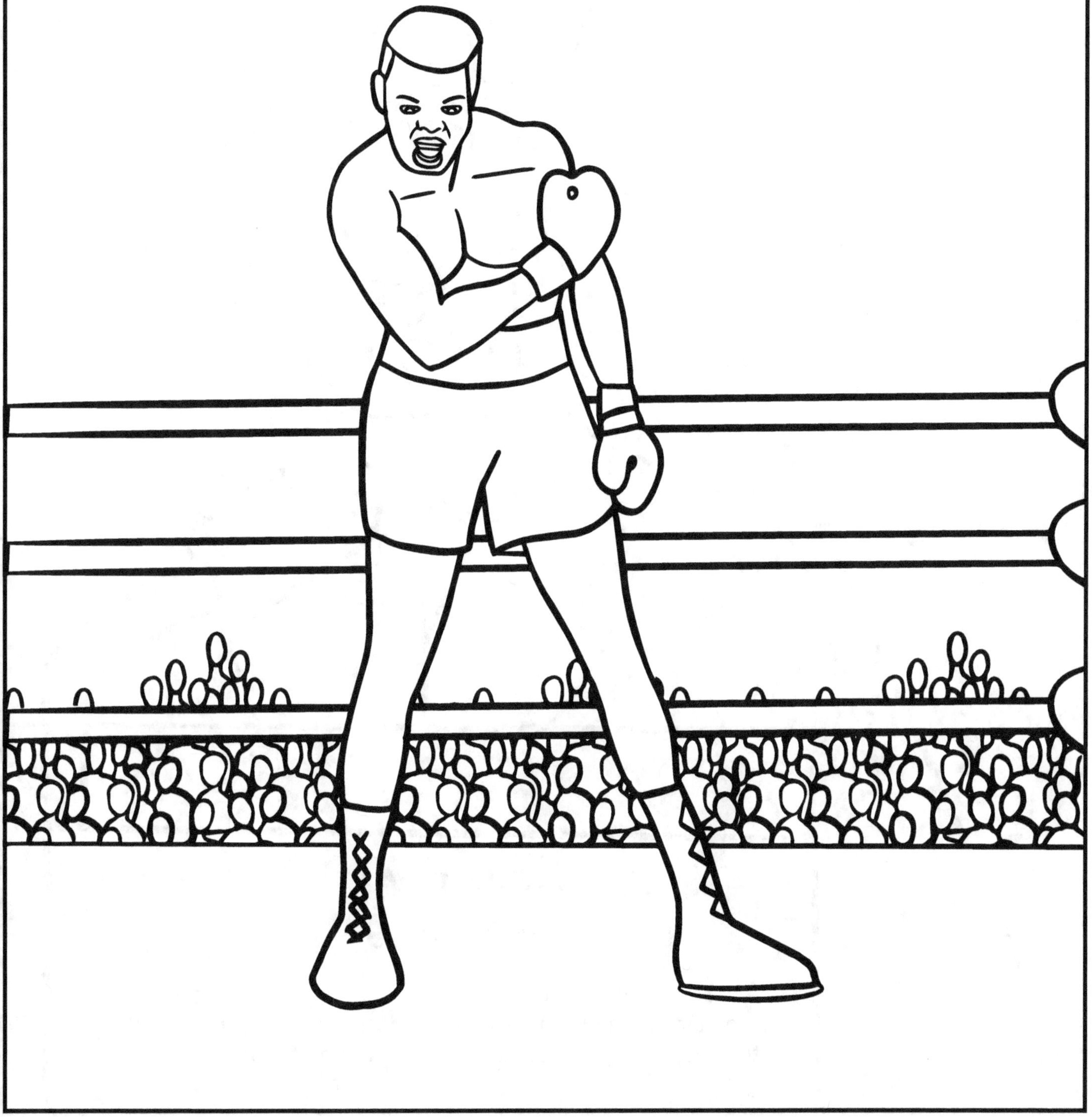

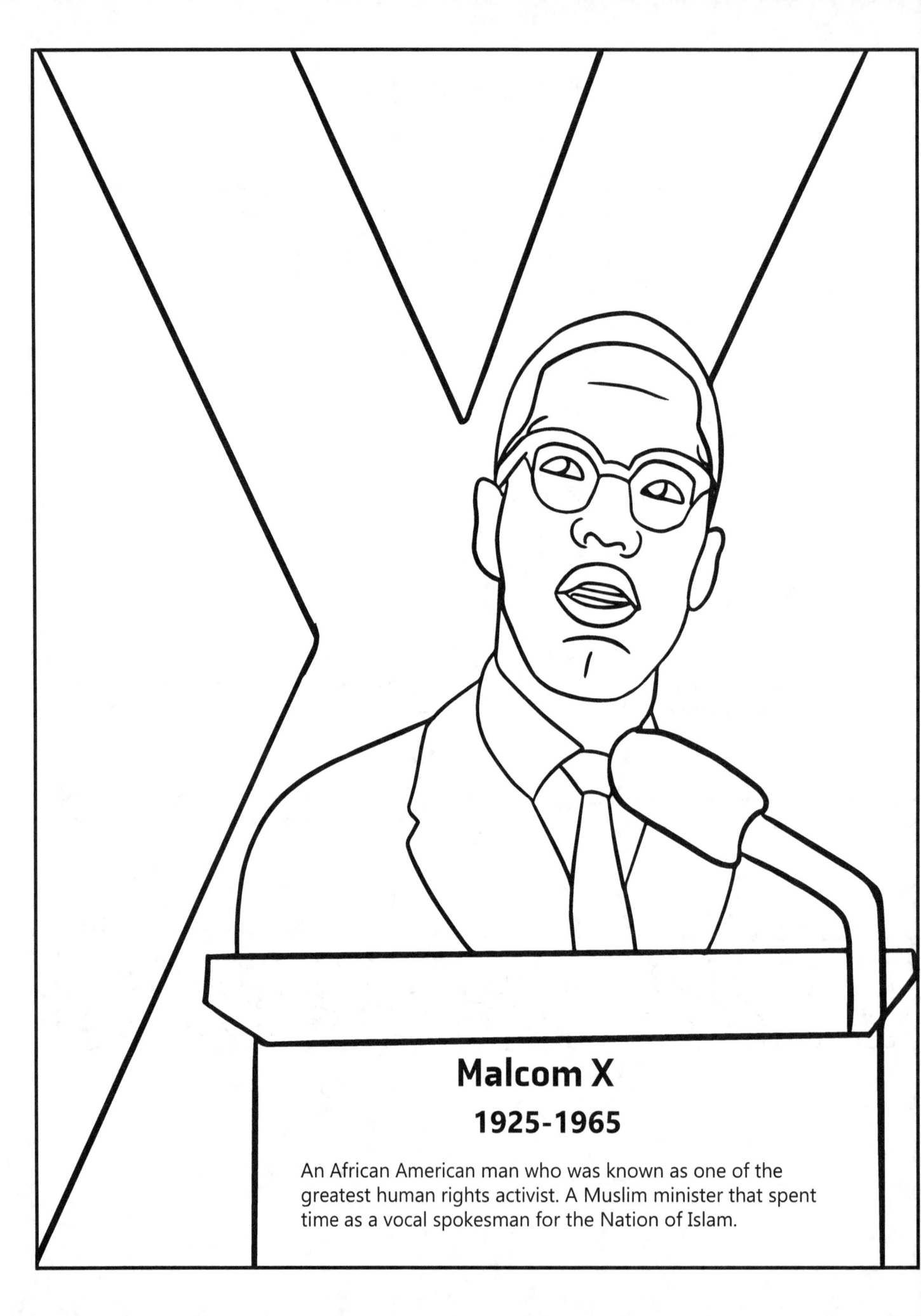

Malcom X

1925-1965

An African American man who was known as one of the greatest human rights activist. A Muslim minister that spent time as a vocal spokesman for the Nation of Islam.

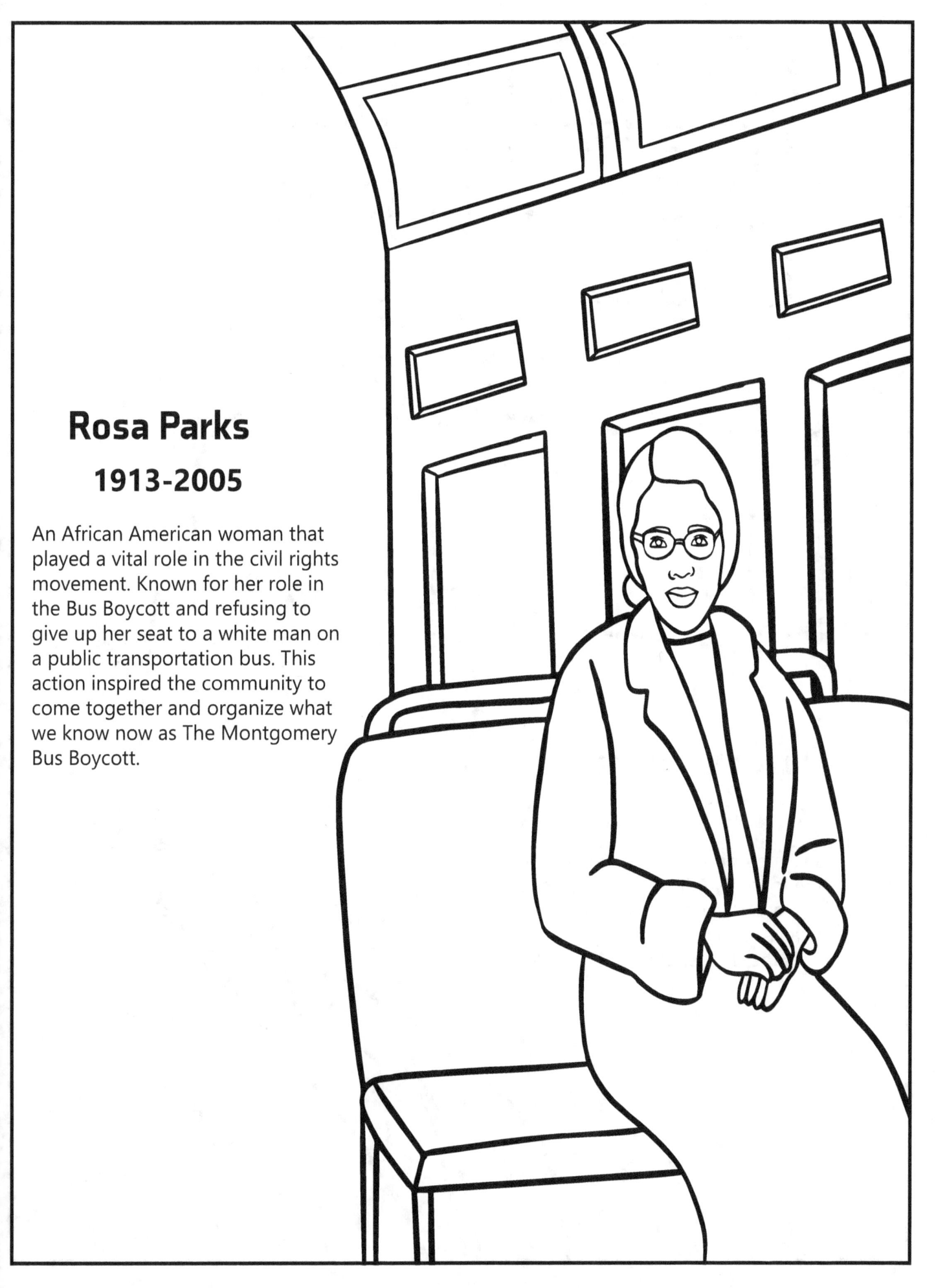

Rosa Parks

1913-2005

An African American woman that played a vital role in the civil rights movement. Known for her role in the Bus Boycott and refusing to give up her seat to a white man on a public transportation bus. This action inspired the community to come together and organize what we know now as The Montgomery Bus Boycott.

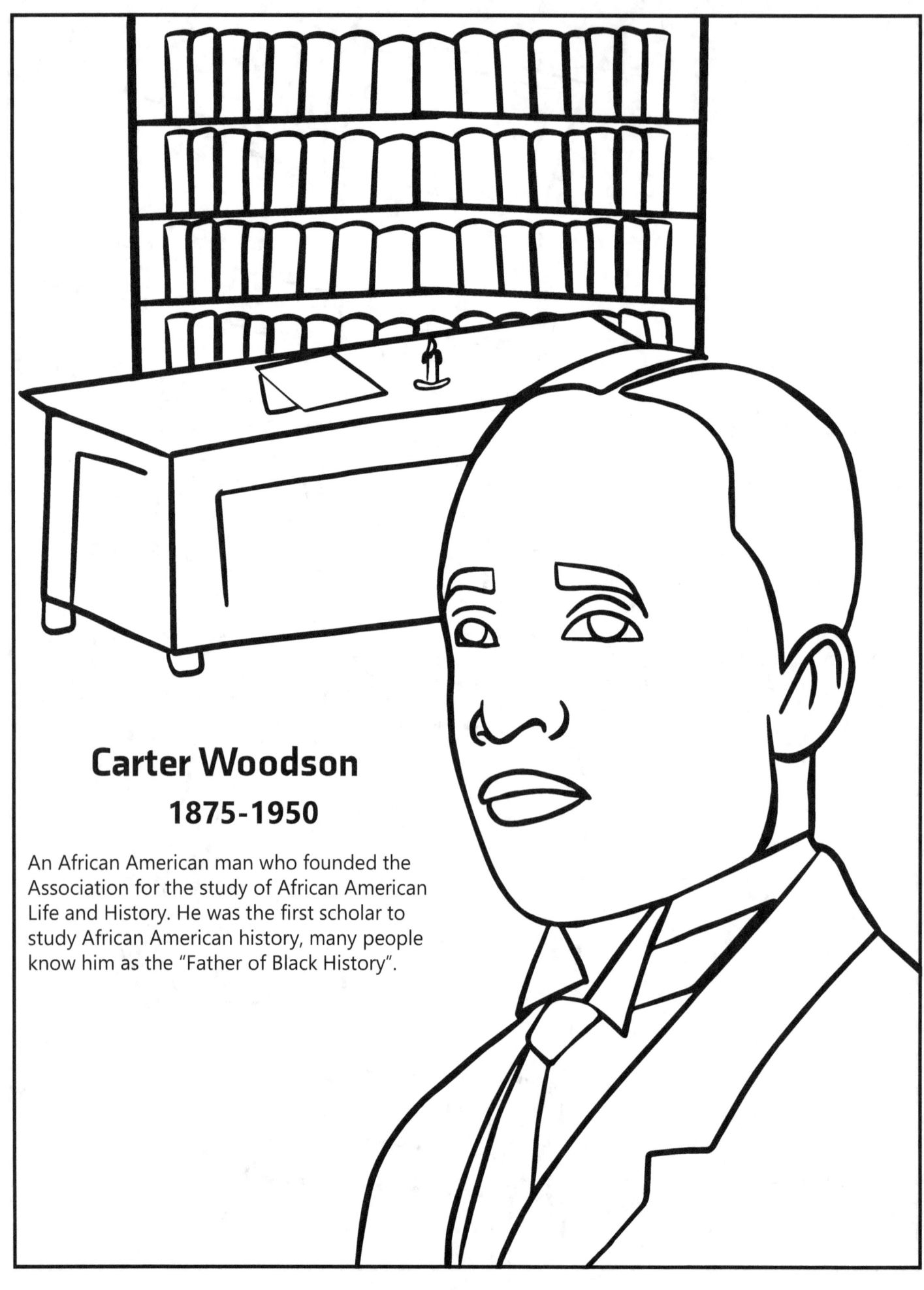

Carter Woodson

1875-1950

An African American man who founded the
Association for the study of African American
Life and History. He was the first scholar to
study African American history, many people
know him as the "Father of Black History".

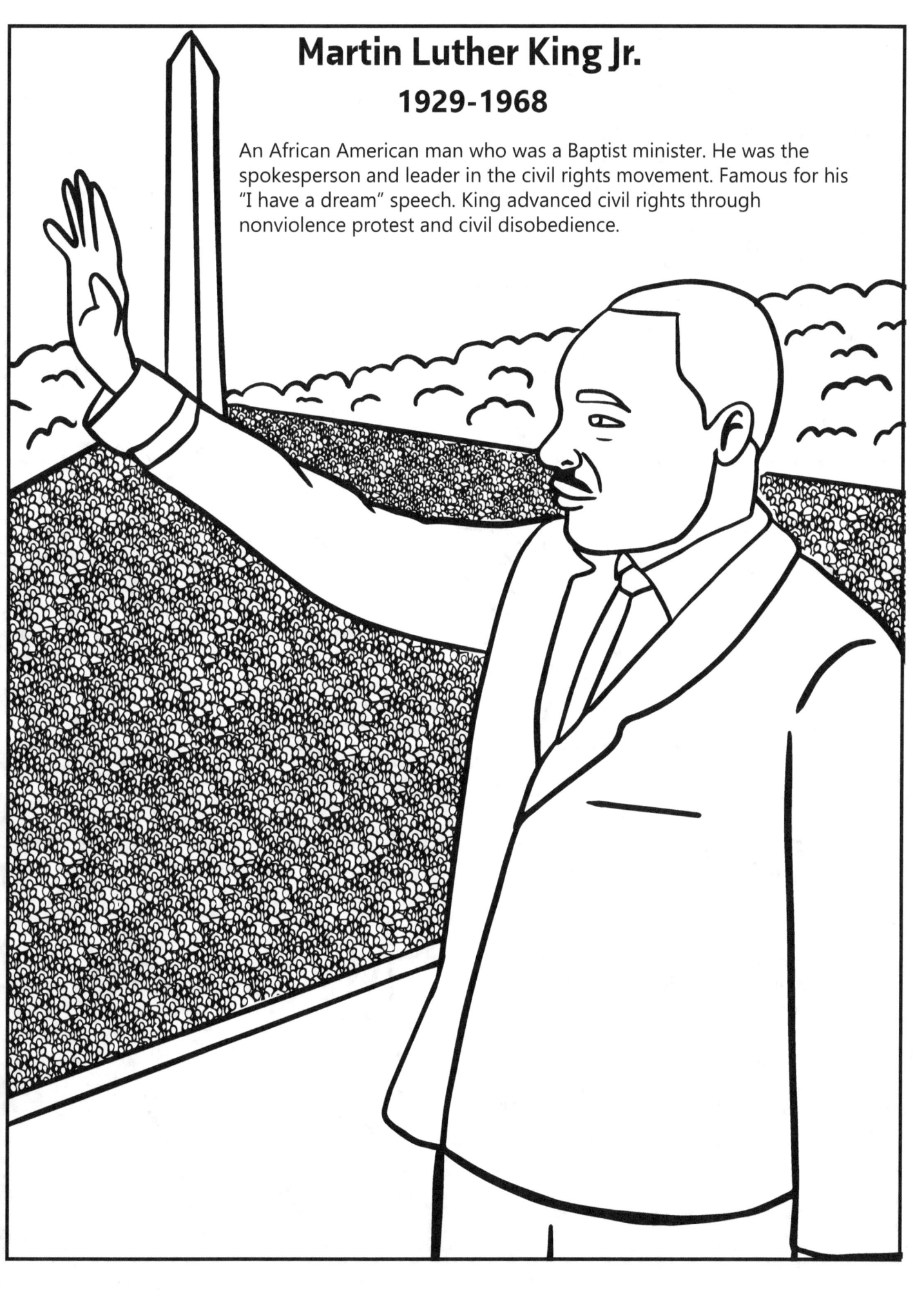

Martin Luther King Jr.

1929-1968

An African American man who was a Baptist minister. He was the spokesperson and leader in the civil rights movement. Famous for his "I have a dream" speech. King advanced civil rights through nonviolence protest and civil disobedience.

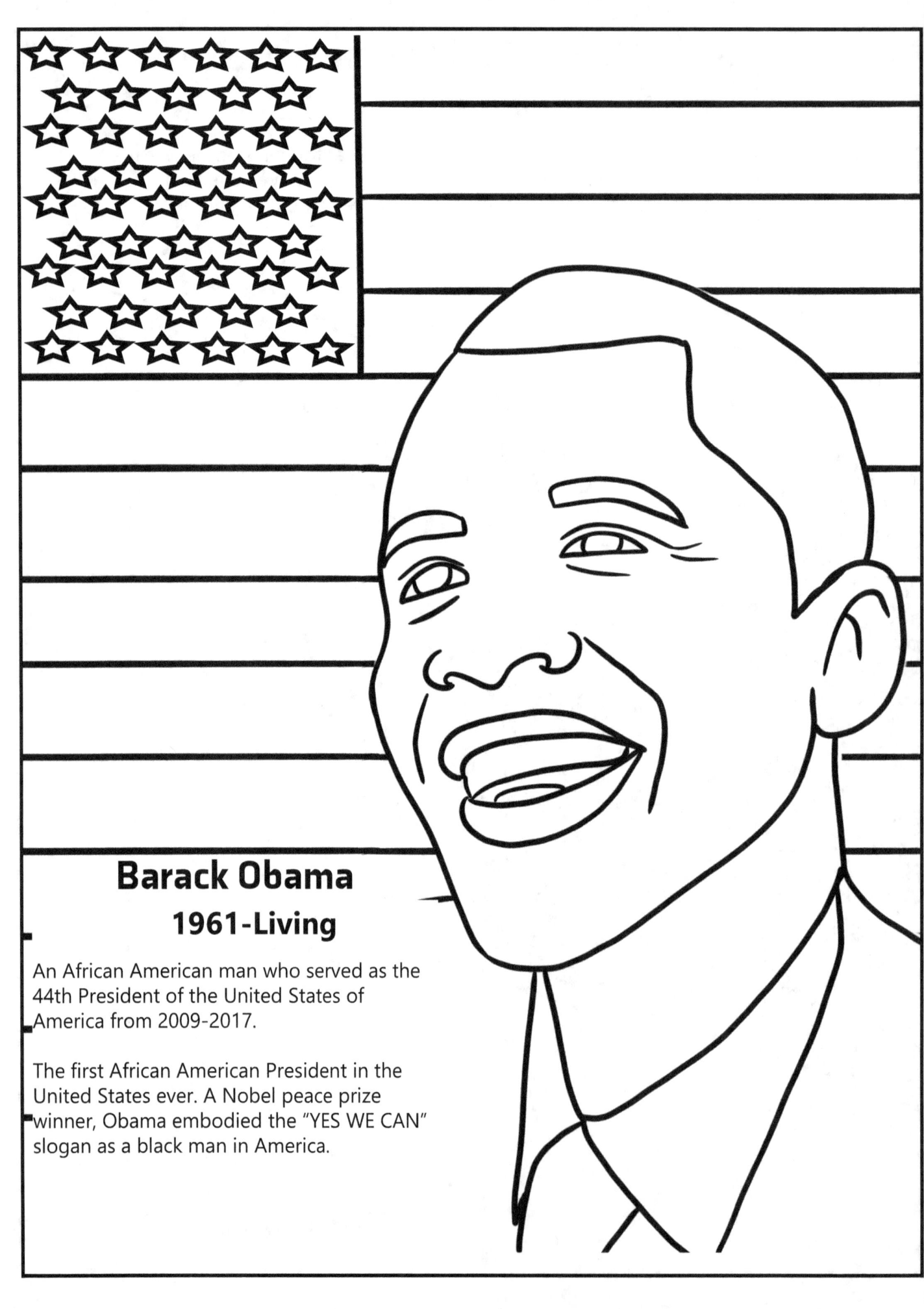

Barack Obama

1961-Living

An African American man who served as the
44th President of the United States of
America from 2009-2017.

The first African American President in the
United States ever. A Nobel peace prize
winner, Obama embodied the "YES WE CAN"
slogan as a black man in America.

What characteristics do you posses that make you a LEADER?

_____

_____

_____

_____

_____

_____

_____

_____

_____

_____

_____

_____

_____

_____

_____

_____

If you were to meet one of your ancestors, what would you say to them?

_____

_____

_____

_____

_____

_____

_____

_____

_____

_____

_____

_____

_____

_____

_____

_____

How has the work of these historical black influencers changed your life?

_____

_____

_____

_____

_____

_____

_____

_____

_____

_____

_____

_____

_____

_____

_____

_____

_____

_____

What would you like to see from black influencers today?

_____

_____

_____

_____

_____

_____

_____

_____

_____

_____

_____

_____

_____

_____

_____

What is at least one thing that makes you proud of your black history?

_____

_____

_____

_____

_____

_____

_____

_____

_____

_____

_____

_____

_____

_____

_____

www.ingramcontent.com/pod-product-compliance
Lightning Source LLC
Chambersburg PA
CBHW082150230526
45467CB00043B/2798